THE ART OF
COCKTAILS

THE ART OF
COCK

MODERN AND CLASSICS

TAILS

THE GUIDE TO STOCKING THE BAR, GLASSWARE, TOOLS, MAKING THE PERFECT COCKTAIL FOR EVERY OCCASION

NH
NEW HOLLAND

C O N T E N T S

INTRODUCTION

METHODS OF MIXING COCKTAILS

The four methods below are the most common
processes of mixing cocktails:

SHAKE • STIR • BUILD • BLEND

SHAKE

To shake is to mix a cocktail by shaking it in a cocktail shaker
by hand. First, fill the glass part of the shaker three quarters
full with ice, then pour the ingredients on top of the ice. Less
expensive ingredients are usually poured before the deluxe
ingredients, just in case you make a mistake! Pour the contents
of the glass into the metal part of the shaker and shake
vigorously for ten to fifteen seconds.

Remove the glass section and using a Hawthorn strainer,
strain contents into the cocktail glass. Shaking ingredients that
do not mix easily with spirits is easy and practical (e.g. juices,
egg whites, cream and sugar syrups).

Most shakers have two or three parts. In a busy bar, the cap
is often temporarily misplaced. If this happens, a coaster or the
inside palm of your hand is quite effective. American shakers
are best.

To sample the cocktail before serving to the customer, pour a small amount into the shaker cap and using a straw check the taste.

STIR

To stir a cocktail is to mix the ingredients by stirring them with ice in a mixing glass and then straining them into a chilled cocktail glass. Short circular twirls are most preferred. (Note: the glass part of a shaker will do well for this.) Spirits, Liqueurs and Vermouths that blend easily together are mixed by this method.

BUILD

To build a cocktail is to mix the ingredients in the glass in which the cocktail is to be served, floating one on top of the other. Hi-ball, long fruit juice and carbonated mixed cocktails are typically built using this technique.

Where possible a swizzle stick should be put into the drink to mix the ingredients after being presented to the customer. Long straws are excellent substitutes when swizzle sticks are unavailable.

BLEND

To blend a cocktail is to mix the ingredients using an electric blender/mixer. It is recommended to add the fruit (fresh or tinned) first. Slicing small pieces gives a smoother texture than if you add the whole fruit. Next, pour the alcohol. Ice should always be added last. This order ensures that the fruit is blended freely with the alcoholic ingredients and allows the ice to gradually mix into the beverage, chilling it. Ideally, the blender should be on for at least 20 seconds.

Following this procedure will prevent ice and fruit lumps that then need to be strained. If the blender starts to rattle and hum, ice may be obstructing the blades from spinning. Always check that the blender is clean before you start. Angostura Bitters is alcohol based which is suitable for cleaning. Fill 4 to 5 shakes with hot water, rinse and then wipe clean.

TECHNIQUES IN MAKING COCKTAILS

SHAKE AND POUR
After shaking the cocktail, pour the contents straight into the glass. When pouring into highball glasses and some old-fashioned glasses the ice cubes are included. This eliminates straining.

SHAKE AND STRAIN
Using a Hawthorn strainer (or knife) this technique prevents the ice going into the glass. Straining protects the cocktail ensuring melted ice won't dilute the mixture.

FLOAT INGREDIENTS
Hold the spoon right way up and rest it with the lip slightly above the level of the last layer. Fill spoon gently and the

contents will flow smoothly from all around the rim. Use the back of the spoon's dish only if you are experienced.

FROSTING (sugar and salt rims)

This technique is used to coat the rim of the glass with either salt or sugar. First, rub lemon/orange slice juice all the way around the glass rim. Next, holding the glass upside down by the stem, rest on a plate containing salt or sugar and turn slightly so that it adheres to the glass. Pressing the glass too deeply into the salt or sugar often results in chunks sticking to the glass. A lemon slice is used for salt and an orange slice is used for sugar.

To achieve colour affects, put a small amount of Grenadine or coloured Liqueur in a plate and coat the rim of the glass, then gently place in the sugar. The sugar absorbs the Grenadine, which turns it pink. This is much easier than mixing Grenadine with sugar and then trying to get it to stick to the glass.

HELPFUL HINTS

Cocktail mixing is an art which is expressed in the preparation and presentation of the cocktail.

STORING FRUIT JUICES
Take an empty wine bottle and soak it in hot water to remove the label and sterilise the alcohol. The glass has excellent appeal and you'll find it easier to pour the correct measurement with an attached nip pourer.

SUGAR SYRUP RECIPE
Sugar syrup is needed in a good cocktail bar as sugar will not dissolve easily in cold cocktails.

Combine equal parts white sugar and boiling water, and keep stirring until the sugar is fully dissolved. Refrigerate when not in use. Putting a teaspoon of sugar into a cocktail is being lazy, it does not do the job properly as the sugar just dissolves.

JUICE TIPS
Never leave juices, coconut cream or other ingredients in cans. Pour them into clean bottles, cap and refrigerate them.

ICE
Ice is probably the most important part of cocktails. It is used in nearly all cocktails. Consequently ice must be clean and fresh at all times.

The small square cubes and flat chips of ice are superior for chilling and mixing cocktails. Ice cubes with holes are inefficient. Wet ice, ice scraps and broken ice should only be used in blenders.

Sour mix

Sour mix, is also known as bar mix, and is an important addition to many cocktails. To make sour mix, whisk one egg white until frothy in a grease-free medium-sized bowl. Mix in 7 oz (200 g) of sugar, followed by 8 fl oz (250 ml) water and 16 fl oz (475 ml) of lemon juice. Beat until the sugar is dissolved. The egg whites are optional, but will make the drinks slightly foamy. Will keep in a refrigerator for about a week.

Note: cocktails, drinks and garnishes containing raw egg are unsuitable for elderly, pregnant women or those who are in ill health.

How to make a decorative cross

Using a sharp knife, find the centre point of a short straw and slice through it. Push another short straw through the slit and position to create a cross. Arrange the cross over the cocktail surface but so it's not touching the liquid. Dusting over the surface with ground (powdered) nutmeg or other sprinkles.

Remove the straw cross to reveal a cross pattern on the drink's surface. Use this technique to create a decorative pattern on the surface of creamy cocktails such as Brandy Alexanders.

CRUSHED ICE

Take the required amount of ice and fold into a clean linen cloth.

Although uncivilized, the most effective method is to smash it against the bar floor. Shattering with a bottle may break the bottle. Some retailers sell portable ice crushers.

Alternatively a blender may be used. Half fill with ice and then pour water into the blender until it reaches the level of the ice. Blend for about 30 seconds, strain out the water and you have perfectly crushed ice. Always try and use a metal scoop to collect the ice from the ice tray.

Never pick up the ice with your hands. This is unhygienic. Shovelling the glass into the ice tray to gather ice can also cause breakages and hence should be avoided where possible.

It is important that the ice tray is cleaned each day. As ice is colourless and odourless, many people assume wrongly it is always clean. Taking a cloth soaked in hot water, wipe the inside of the bucket.

BAR GLASSWARE

Highball · Zombie · Collins · Weizenbier · Pilsner

Old Fashioned · Rocks · Tumbler · Cosmopolitan · Martini

Red Wine · White Wine · Rose Wine · Port Wine · Sherry

Snifter · Wobble · Tulip · Nosing · Pousse Cafe

GLASSES

Brandy balloon

Champagne flute

Coupe

Highball

Hurricane

Glass coffee cup

Margarita

Martini glass

Old fashioned

A proven method to polishing glasses once clean is to hold each glass individually over a bucket of boiling water until the glass becomes steamy and then with a clean linen cloth rub in a circular way to ensure the glass is polished for the next serve.

Cocktails can be poured into any glass but the better the glass the better the appearance of the cocktail.

One basic rule should apply and that is, use no coloured glasses as they spoil the appearance of cocktails.

All glasses have been designed for a specific task, e.g., **Highball** glasses for long cool refreshing drinks. **Martini** glasses for short, sharp, or stronger drinks. **Champagne** saucers for creamy after-dinner style drinks, etc. The stem of the glass has been designed so you may hold it whilst polishing, leaving the bowl free of marks and germs so that you may enjoy your drink.

All cocktail glasses should be kept in a refrigerator or filled with ice while you are preparing the cocktails in order to chill the glass.

An appealing affect on a 90 ml cocktail glass can be achieved by running the glass under cold water and then placing it in the freezer.

Champagne saucer: 140 ml (4⅔ fl oz) – 180 ml (6 fl oz)

Cocktail: 90 ml (3 fl oz) – 140 ml (4⅔ fl oz)

Goblet: 140 ml (4⅔ fl oz) – 285 ml (9½ fl oz)

Hurricane: 230 ml (7⅔ fl oz) – 650 ml (21⅔ fl oz)

Margarita: 260 ml (8⅔ fl oz)

GARNISHES AND JUICES

Almonds

Apple juice

Apricot conserve

Banana

Blueberries

Carbonated water

Celery

Celery salt

Chocolate flakes

Cinnamon

Cocktail onions

Coconut cream

Cream

Crushed pineapple

Cucumber

Edible flowers

Eggs

Jelly babies

Lemon juice

Lemons

Lime juice

Limes

Milk

Mint leaves

Nutmeg

Olives

Orange and mango juice

Orange juice

Oranges

Pepper

Pineapple

Pineapple juice

Red cocktail onions

Red maraschino cherries

Rockmelon

Salt

Strawberries

Sugar

Sugar cubes

Sugar syrup

Tabasco sauce

Tinned fruit/pulps

Tinned nectars

Tomato

Vanilla ice cream

Worcestershire sauce

Simplicity is the most important fact to keep in mind when garnishing cocktails. Do not overdo the garnish; make it striking, but if you can't get near the cocktail to drink it then you have failed. Most world champion cocktails just have a lemon slice, or a single red cherry.

Tall refreshing highballs tend to have more garnish as the glass is larger. A swizzle stick should nearly always be served in long cocktails.

Plastic animals, umbrellas, fans and a whole variety of novelty goods are now available to garnish with, and they add a lot of fun to the drink.

ESSENTIAL EQUIPMENT

ESSENTIAL EQUIPMENT FOR A COCKTAIL BAR

- Bottle openers
- Can-opener
- Coasters and serviettes
- Cocktail shaker
- Free pourers
- Hand cloths for cleaning glasses
- Hawthorn strainer
- Ice bucket
- Ice scoop
- Knife, cutting board
- Measures (jiggers)
- Mixing glass
- Moulinex electric blender
- Scooper spoon (long teaspoon)
- Spoon with muddler
- Swizzle sticks, straws
- Waiter's friend corkscrew

ALCOHOLS

ALCOHOL RECOMMENDED FOR A COCKTAIL BAR

SPIRITS
Bourbon
Brandy
Campari
Canadian club
Gin
Malibu
Ouzo
Pernod
Rum
Scotch
Southern Comfort
Tennessee Whisky
Tequila
Vodka

VERMOUTH
Cinzano Bianco
Martini Bianco
Cinzano Dry
Martini Dry
Cinzano Rosso
Martini Rosso

LIQUEURS

Advocaat
Amaretto
Bailey's Irish Cream
Banana Liqueur
Benedictine
Blue Curaçao
Cassis
Chartreuse –
    green and yellow
Cherry Advocaat
Cherry Brandy
Clayton's tonic (non-alcoholic)
Coconut Liqueur
Cointreau
Crème de café
Crème de menthe – green
Dark Crème de Cacao
Drambuie
Frangelico
Galliano
Grand Marnier
Kahlúa
Kirsch
Mango Liqueur
Melon Liqueur
Pimm's
Sambuca – clear
Sambuca – black
Strawberry Liqueur
Triple Sec

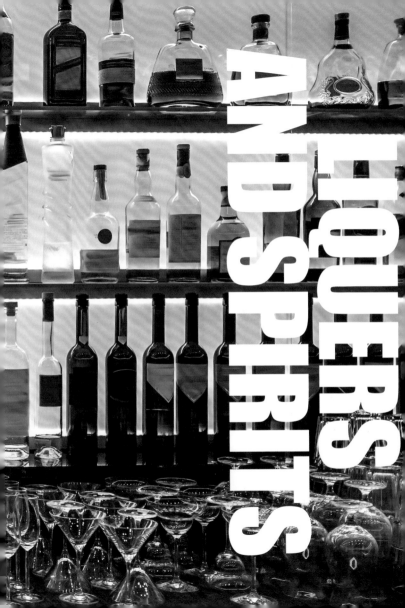

LIQUERS AND SPIRITS

DESCRIPTION OF LIQUEURS AND SPIRITS

Advocaat
A combination of fresh egg whites, yolks, sugar, brandy, vanilla and spirit. Limited shelf life. Recommended shelf life 12–15 months from date of manufacture.

Amaretto
A rich subtle Liqueur with a unique almond taste.

Angostura Bitters
An essential part of any bar or kitchen. A unique additive whose origins date back to 1824. A mysterious blend of natural herbs and spices, it is a seasoning agent in both sweet and savoury dishes and drinks. Ideal for dieters as it is low in sodium and calories.

Bailey's Irish Cream
The largest selling Liqueur in the world. It is a blend of Irish Whisky, softened by Irish Cream. It is a natural product.

Banana Liqueur
Fresh ripe bananas are the perfect base for the definitive daiquiri and a host of other exciting fruit cocktails.

Benedictine
A perfect end to a perfect meal. Serve straight, with ice, soda, or as part of a favourite cocktail.

Bourbon
Has a smooth, deep, easy taste.

Brandy
Smooth and mild spirit, is considered very smooth and palatable, ideal for mixing.

Campari
A drink for many occasions, both as a long or short drink, or as a key ingredient in many fashionable cocktails.

Cassis
Deep, rich purple promises and delivers a regal and robust taste and aroma. Cassis lends itself to neat drinking or an endless array of delicious sauces and desserts.

Chartreuse
A Liqueur available in either yellow or green colour. Made by the monks of the Carthusian order. The only world famous Liqueur still made by monks.

Cherry Advocaat
Same as Advocaat, infused with natural cherry.

Cherry Brandy
Made from concentrated, morello cherry juice. Small quantity of bitter almonds and vanilla is added to make it more enjoyable as a neat drink before or after dinner. Excellent for mixers, topping, ice cream, fruit salads, pancakes, etc.

Coconut Liqueur
A smooth Liqueur, composed of exotic coconut, heightened with light-bodied White Rum.

Cointreau
Made from a neutral grain Spirit, as opposed to Cognac. An aromatic taste of natural citrus fruits. A great mixer or delightful over ice.

Crème de Cacao – dark
Rich, deep chocolate. Smooth and classy. Serve on its own, or mix for all kinds of delectable treats.

Kirsch

A fruit Brandy distilled from morello cherries. Delicious drunk straight and excellent in a variety of food recipes.

Drambuie

A Scotch Whisky Liqueur. Made from a secret recipe dating back to 1745. "Dram Buidheach" the drink that satisfies.

Frangelico

A precious Liqueur imported from Italy. Made from wild hazelnuts with infusions of berries and flowers to enrich the taste.

Grand Marnier

An original blend of fine old cognac and an extract of oranges. The recipe is over 150 years old.

Kahlúa

A smooth, dark Liqueur made from real coffee and fine clear spirits. Its origins are based in Mexico.

Malibu

A clear Liqueur based on White Rum with the subtle addition of Coconut. Its distinctive taste blends naturally with virtually every mixer available.

Melon Liqueur

Soft green, exudes freshness. Refreshing and mouth-watering honeydew melon. Simple yet complex. Smooth on the palate, serve on the rocks, or use to create summertime cocktails.

Ouzo

The traditional spirit aperitif of Greece. The distinctive taste is derived mainly from the seed of the anise plant. A neutral grain spirit.

Peach Schnapps

Crystal clear, light Liqueur, bursting with the taste of ripe peaches. Drink chilled, on the rocks or mix with any soft drink or juice.

Rum

A smooth, dry, light bodied Rum, especially suited for drinks in which you require subtle aroma and delicate taste.

Rye Whiskey

Distilled from corn, rye and malted barley. A light, mild and delicate Whiskey, ideal for drinking straight or in mixed cocktails.

Sambuca – clear

The Italian electric taste experience. Made from elder berries with a touch of anise.

Sambuca – black

An exciting encounter between Sambuca di Galliano and extracts of black elderberry.

Scotch Whisky

A Whisky made in Scotland based on malt or grain. Similar taste to Bourbon but with an added bite.

Southern Comfort

A Liqueur not a Bourbon as often thought. It is a unique, full-bodied Liqueur with a touch of sweetness. Its recipe is a secret, but it is known to be based on peaches and apricots.

Strawberry Liqueur

Fluorescent red, unmistakable strawberry bouquet. Natural Liqueur delivers a true to nature, fresh strawberry taste.

Tennessee Whiskey

Contrary to popular belief, this is not a Bourbon, it is a distinctive product called Tennessee Whiskey. Made from the 'old sour mash' process. Leached through hard maple charcoal, then aged in charred white oak barrels, at a controlled temperature, acquiring body, bouquet and colour, yet remaining smooth.

Tequila

Distilled from the Mexcal variety of the cacti plant. A perfect mixer or drink straight with salt and lemon.

Tia Maria

A Liqueur with a cane spirit base, and its taste derived from the finest Jamaican coffee. It is not too sweet with a subtle taste of coffee.

Triple Sec

Triple sec is an orange-flavoured Liqueur that originated in France.

Vermouth

By description, Vermouth is a herbally infused wine. Three styles are most prevalent, these are:

Rosso – A bitter sweet herbal taste, often drunk as an aperitif.

Bianco – Is light, fruity and refreshing. Mixes well with soda, lemonade and fruit juices.

Dry – Is crisp, light and dry and is used as a base for many cocktails.

Vodka

The second largest selling spirit in the world. Most vodkas are steeped in tanks containing charcoal, removing all odours and impurities, making a superior quality product.

Crème de Cacao – white

This Liqueur delivers a powerfully lively, full bodied chocolate taste. Excellent ingredient when absence of colour is desired.

Crème de menthe – green

Clear peppermint flavour, reminiscent of a fresh, crisp, clean winter's day in the mountains. Excellent mixer, a necessity in the gourmet kitchen.

Crème de menthe – white

As Crème de menthe – green, when colour is not desired.

Curaçao – blue

Same as Triple Sec, brilliant blue colour is added to make some cocktails more exciting.

Curaçao – Orange

Again, same as above, but stronger in orange, colouring is used for other varieties of cocktail mixers.

Curaçao Triple Sec

Based on natural citrus fruits. Well known fact is citrus fruits are the most important aromatic taste constituents. As a Liqueur one of the most versatile. Can be enjoyed with or without ice as a neat drink, or used in mixed cocktails more than any other Liqueur. Triple Sec – also known as White Curaçao.

Galliano – Vanilla

The distinguished taste! A classic Liqueur that blends with a vast array of mixed drinks.

Gin

Its aroma comes from using the highest quality juniper berries and other rare and subtle herbs. Perfect mixer for both short and long drinks.

RUM

COLADA

The history of the Colada began with the creation of the Piña Colada in 1954. The Piña Colada was created by Ramon 'Monchito' Marrero whilst he was a bartender at the Caribe Hilton Hotel in San Juan, Puerto Rico. Ramon Marrero wanted to combine the flavors of Puerto Rico into a drink. Piña Colada was declared to be the national drink of Puerto Rico in 1978. Piña Colada translates in Spanish as 'strained pineapple'.

Today there are many varieties of Colada cocktails, with the majority containing light rum, coconut cream and pineapple juice which are served in hurricane glasses.

MELON COLADA

38 ml (1¼ fl oz) Light Rum
38 ml (1¼ fl oz) Midori
90 ml (3 fl oz) pineapple juice
40 ml (1⅓ fl oz) coconut cream (chilled)
1 teaspoon thick cream (chilled)
Garnish: maraschino cherry
Garnish: slice of fresh pineapple

- Pour Rum, Midori, juice and creams into a blender over a large amount of crushed ice.

- Blend until slushy and pour into a chilled hurricane glass.

- Garnish with a maraschino cherry and a slice of pineapple then serve.

PIÑA COLADA

60 ml (2 fl oz) Jamaican Rum
60 ml (2 fl oz) pineapple juice
60 ml (2 fl oz) thick cream (chilled)
30 ml (1 fl oz) coconut milk (chilled)
Maraschino cherry
Garnish: slice of fresh pineapple

- Pour Rum, juice, thick cream and coconut milk into a blender over a large amount of crushed ice. Blend until slushy and pour into a chilled hurricane or large glass.

- Garnish with a maraschino cherry and a slice of pineapple then serve.

- This drink may also be prepared in a cocktail shaker over a large amount of crushed ice if preferred.

STRAWBERRY COLADA

38 ml (1¼ fl oz) Light Rum
38 ml (1¼ fl oz) Strawberry Liqueur
90 ml (3 fl oz) pineapple juice
40 ml (1⅓ fl oz) coconut cream
   (chilled)
1 teaspoon thick cream (chilled)
2 fresh strawberries (diced)
Garnish: fresh fruit or strawberries

- Pour Rum, Liqueur, juice and creams
  into a blender over a large amount
  of crushed ice then add diced
  strawberries.

- Blend until slushy and pour into a
  chilled hurricane glass.

- Garnish with fresh fruit and then
  serve.

STRAWBERRY COLADA

GINGER COLADA

23 ml (¾ fl oz) Dark Rum
15 ml (½ fl oz) Ginger Brandy
120 ml (4 fl oz) pineapple juice
30 ml (1 fl oz) coconut cream (chilled)

- Pour Rum, Ginger Brandy, juice and coconut cream into a blender over a large amount of crushed ice.

- Blend until slushy and pour into a chilled hurricane glass.

- Garnish with fresh fruit if desired then serve.

BANANA COLADA

38 ml (1¼ fl oz) Light Rum
38 ml (1¼ fl oz) Banana Liqueur
90 ml (3 fl oz) pineapple juice
40 ml (1⅓ fl oz) coconut cream (chilled)
1 teaspoon thick cream (chilled)
1 fresh banana (diced)
Garnish: maraschino cherry
Garnish: slice of banana
Garnish: slice of fresh pineapple

- Pour Rum, Liqueur, juice and creams into a blender over a large amount of crushed ice then add diced banana.

- Blend until slushy and pour into a chilled hurricane glass.

- Garnish with a maraschino cherry, slice of banana and a slice of pineapple then serve.

APPLE COLADA

38 ml (1¼ fl oz) Light Rum
38 ml (1¼ fl oz) Apple Schnapps
90 ml (3 fl oz) pineapple juice
40 ml (1⅓ fl oz) coconut cream (chilled)
1 teaspoon thick cream (chilled)

- Pour Rum, Schnapps, juice and creams into a blender over a large amount of crushed ice then blend until slushy.

- Pour into a chilled hurricane glass then garnish with fresh fruit of your choice.

APPLE COLADA

COFFEE COLADA

38 ml (1¼ fl oz) Light Rum
38 ml (1¼ fl oz) Tia Maria
90 ml (3 fl oz) pineapple juice
40 ml (1⅓ fl oz) coconut cream
  (chilled)
1 teaspoon thick cream (chilled)
Garnish: maraschino cherry
Garnish: slice of fresh pineapple

- Pour Rum, Tia Maria, juice and creams into a blender over a large amount of crushed ice.

- Blend until slushy and pour into a chilled hurricane glass.

- Garnish with a maraschino cherry and a slice of pineapple then serve.

COCOA COLADA

45 ml (1½ fl oz) Light Rum
15 ml (½ fl oz) Coconut Liqueur
8 ml (¼ fl oz) Kahlúa
45 ml (1½ fl oz) fresh milk (chilled)
15 ml (½ fl oz) chocolate syrup
Pinch of grated chocolate

- Pour Rum, Liqueur, Kahlúa, milk and chocolate syrup into a blender over a large amount of crushed ice then blend until slushy.

- Pour into a chilled hurricane glass and sprinkle grated chocolate on top.

STRAWBERRY BANANA COLADA

38 ml (1¼ fl oz) Light Rum
60 ml (2 fl oz) coconut cream (chilled)
6 fresh strawberries (diced)
1 fresh banana (diced)
Garnish: slice of fresh banana
Garnish: fresh strawberry

- Pour Rum and coconut cream into a blender over a large amount of crushed ice.

- Add diced strawberries and diced banana then blend until slushy.

- Pour into a chilled hurricane glass then garnish with slices of banana and strawberry. Serve with a straw.

CLASSIC DAIQUIRI

45 ml (1½ fl oz) Bacardi
5 ml (⅙ fl oz) Grenadine
15 ml (½ fl oz) fresh lime juice

- Pour ingredients into a cocktail shaker over ice and shake.

- Strain into a chilled cocktail glass and serve.

CLASSIC DAIQUIRI

FROZEN DAIQUIRI

60 ml (2 fl oz) Bacardi
45 ml (1½ fl oz) lime juice
30 ml (1 fl oz) sugar syrup
Garnish: lemon wedges

- Pour ingredients over a two handfuls of crushed ice and blend until smooth then pour into chilled glass.

- Sometimes the taste of this drink can be diluted by blending it over ice. For a more intense drink, try using either a Dark Rum or a dark sugar syrup.

Variations

- Mango Daiquiri: replace half the Rum with 15 ml (½ fl oz) Cointreau and 15 ml (½ fl oz) Mango Liqueur, and add half a diced fresh Mango before blending. Banana Daiquiri: replace a quarter of the Rum with 15 ml(½ fl oz) Banana Liqueur, and add half a diced.

BACARDI DAIQUIRI

45 ml (1½ fl oz) Bacardi
5 ml (⅙ fl oz) Grenadine
15 ml (½ fl oz) fresh lemon or lime juice
1 teaspoon egg white
Garnish: maraschino cherry

- Pour Bacardi, Grenadine, lemon or lime juice as desired and egg white into a cocktail shaker over ice then shake well.

- Strain into a chilled cocktail glass and garnish with a maraschino cherry then serve.

BACARDI DAIQUIRI

STRAWBERRY DAIQUIRI

30 ml (1 fl oz) Bacardi
15 ml (½ fl oz) Cointreau
15 ml (½ fl oz) Strawberry Liqueur
30 ml (1 fl oz) fresh lemon juice
4 fresh strawberries (diced)
Garnish: fresh strawberry

- Pour Bacardi, Cointreau, Liqueur
  and juice into a blender over small
  amount of crushed ice then add
  diced strawberries.

- Blend until smooth and pour into a
  chilled cocktail glass.

- Garnish with a strawberry and serve.

STRAWBERRY DAIQUIRI

MANGO DAIQUIRI

30 ml (1 fl oz) Bacardi
15 ml (½ fl oz) Cointreau
15 ml (½ fl oz) Mango Liqueur
30 ml (1 fl oz) fresh lemon juice
1 fresh Mango (diced)
Garnish: slice of fresh Mango

- Pour Bacardi, Cointreau, Liqueur and juice into a blender over a small amount of crushed ice then add diced Mango.

- Blend until smooth and pour into a chilled cocktail glass.

- Garnish with a slice of Mango and serve with a straw.

MANGO DAIQUIRI

PEACH DAIQUIRI

45 ml (1½ fl oz) Bacardi
15 ml (½ fl oz) Peach Liqueur
30 ml (1 fl oz) fresh lemon juice
1 fresh Peach (diced)
Garnish: slice of fresh Peach

- Pour Bacardi, Liqueur and juice into a blender over a small amount of crushed ice then add diced Peach.

- Blend until smooth and pour into a chilled cocktail glass.

- Garnish with a slice of Peach and serve with a short straw.

ROCKMELON DAIQUIRI

45 ml (1½ fl oz) Bacardi
30 ml (1 fl oz) Cointreau
20 ml (⅔ fl oz) Mango Liqueur
20 ml (⅔ fl oz) fresh lemon juice
⅓ fresh Rockmelon (diced)

- Pour Bacardi, Cointreau, Liqueur
  and juice into a blender over a small
  amount of crushed ice then add
  diced Rockmelon.

- Blend until smooth and pour into
  a chilled cocktail glass then serve
  with a short straw.

DAIQUIRI COCKTAIL

45 ml (1½ fl oz) Bacardi
30 ml (1 fl oz) fresh lime juice
1 teaspoon sugar syrup

- Pour ingredients into a cocktail shaker over ice and shake.

- Strain into a chilled cocktail glass and serve with a short green straw.

PINEAPPLE DAIQUIRI

60 ml (2 fl oz) Bacardi
15 ml (½ fl oz) Cointreau
15 ml (½ fl oz) fresh lemon juice
15 ml (½ fl oz) fresh lime juice
6 pieces of fresh pineapple (diced)
Garnish: slice of fresh pineapple

- Pour Bacardi, Cointreau and juices into a blender over a small amount of crushed ice then add diced pineapple.

- Blend until smooth and pour into a chilled cocktail glass.

- Garnish with a slice of pineapple and serve with a short yellow straw.

KIWI DAIQUIRI

30 ml (1 fl oz) Bacardi
15 ml (½ fl oz) Cointreau
15 ml (½ fl oz) Midori
15 ml (½ fl oz) fresh lime juice
½ teaspoon sugar syrup
½ fresh Kiwi fruit (diced)
Garnish: slice of fresh kiwifruit

- Pour Bacardi, Cointreau, Midori, juice and sugar into a blender over a small amount of crushed ice then add diced kiwifruit.

- Blend until smooth and pour into a chilled cocktail glass. Garnish with a slice of kiwifruit and serve with a short green straw.

MAI TAI

30 ml (1 fl oz) Rum
15 ml (½ fl oz) Dark Rum
30 ml (1 fl oz) Orange Curaçao
15 ml (½ fl oz) Amaretto
30 ml (1 fl oz) sugar syrup
30 ml (1 fl oz) lemon juice
½ fresh lime, juiced

- Pour ingredients into a cocktail shaker over ice and shake.

- Strain over fresh ice.

- Grenadine is often added to redden a glowing effect while the Rum may be floated on top when served without straws.

- Garnish: pineapple spear, orange slice, mint leaves, tropical flowers if desired and limes all optional.

MAI TAI

MOJITO

60 ml (2 fl oz) Light Rum
30 ml (1 fl oz) fresh lime juice
½ teaspoon sugar syrup
60 ml (2 fl oz) soda water
6 Sprigs of fresh mint
Garnish: mint

- Pour sugar into a chilled collins glass and add 2–3 sprigs of mint. Muddle well and add juice.

- Add crushed ice to half fill glass and stir. Add Rum and stir. Add more crushed ice and soda then stir gently.

- Garnish with sprigs of mint placed vertically in drink and serve.

LONG ISLAND ICED TEA

30 ml (1 fl oz) Vodka
30 ml (1 fl oz) White Rum
30 ml (1 fl oz) Cointreau
30 ml (1 fl oz) Tequila
30 ml (1 fl oz) Gin
30 ml (1 fl oz) lemon juice
Dash of Cola
30 ml (1 fl oz) sugar syrup

- Pour all ingredients except for Cola into a cocktail shaker over ice and shake. Strain over fresh ice and top with Cola.

- The tea-coloured Cola is splashed into the cocktail making it slightly unsuitable for a 'tea party'.

HURRICANE

30 ml (1 fl oz) Bacardi
30 ml (1 fl oz) orange juice
15 ml (½ fl oz) lime cordial
45 ml (1½ fl oz) lemon juice
45 ml (1½ fl oz) sugar syrup
15 ml Bacardi Gold, to top
Garnish: orange slice and cherry

- Pour all ingredients except for Bacardi Gold into a cocktail shaker over ice and shake.

- Strain over fresh ice and gently float Bacardi Gold on top.

- Garnish: orange slice and cherry.

MINT JULEP

60 ml (2 fl oz) Bourbon
10 ml (⅓ fl oz) sugar syrup
2–3 dashes cold water or soda water
8 sprigs of fresh mint
Crushed or shaved ice
Garnish: mint

- Muddle sugar syrup and 5 mint sprigs in a glass until the mint becomes fragrant, but stop before it breaks up.

- Pour into thoroughly frosted glass and pack with ice. Add Bourbon and water/soda and mix (with a chopping motion using a longhandled bar spoon).

- Garnish with remaining mint and serve with a straw.

OLD FASHIONED

60 ml (2 fl oz) Bourbon or Rye Whiskey
2 dashes Bitters
Sugar cube
Garnish: twist of orange peel, cherry,
   and an oversized ice cube

- Place sugar cube in glass, coat with
  Bitters and muddle. Add Whiskey
  and stir until sugar is completely
  dissolved.

- Add oversized ice cube and squeeze
  orange peel over the glass to release
  the oils before dropping in the drink.

Variations

RUM OLD FASHIONED

- Replace Bourbon/Rye with 60 ml
  (2 fl oz) brown Rum.

CARIBBEAN MARTINI

Lime slice
Granulated (white) sugar
45 ml (1½ fl oz) Light Rum
7.5 ml (1½ tsp) Dry Vermouth
Garnish: lime twist

- Run the lime slice around the rim of a chilled cocktail glass.

- Coat with sugar. Combine the liquid ingredients with ice in a cocktail shaker and shake well. Strain into the glass and garnish with the lime twist.

ESPRESSO MARTINI

30 ml freshly brewed Espresso coffee
30 ml Vodka
30 ml Kahlua
5 ml sugar syrup (optional)
Garnish: 3 coffee beans

- Pour ingredients into a cocktail shaker over ice and shake vigorously. Double strain into chilled glass.

- Mixture must be shaken hard and strained/ poured immediately to create the crema that sits on top of the cocktail.

Variations

ESPRESSO MARTINI FRANGELICO

• Replace Kahlua with 30 ml Frangelico.

ESPRESSO MARTINI VANILLA

• Either replace Vodka with Vanilla Vodka, or use the following proportions: 30 ml fresh Espresso, 20 ml Vodka, 20 ml Kahlua, 20 ml Vanilla Galliano. Salted caramel. Replace half the Kahlua with 15 ml Vanilla Galliano. Replace sugar syrup with 15 ml salted caramel syrup.

ESPRESSO MARTINI RUM

• Replace Vodka with spiced Rum.

ESPRESSO MARTINI IRISH

• Replace Vodka with Jamesons.

ESPRESSO MARTINI

BLOODY MARY

60 ml (2 fl oz) Vodka
120 ml (4 fl oz) tomato juice
Salt and pepper to taste
Worcestershire sauce to taste
Celery salt, optional
Tabasco sauce to taste
Lemon juice to taste
Garnish: celery stalk, lemon slice

- Pour ingredients into a mixing glass over ice and stir. Strain into glass and serve.

- Remember to add the spices first, then Vodka and lemon juice followed by tomato juice. The celery stick is not just part of the garnish, so feel free to nibble as you drink.

- The glass may also be salt-rimmed.

- Feel free to play around with the garnish, suggestions include cucumber, olives, cherry tomatoes – anything you like!

BLOODY MARY

COSMOPOLITAN

COSMOPOLITAN

45 ml (1½ fl oz) Absolut Citron Vodka
20 ml (⅓ fl oz) Triple sec
20 ml (⅔ fl oz) cranberry juice
Juice of ½ fresh lime
Garnish: orange twist

- Pour ingredients into a cocktail shaker over ice and shake.

- Strain into chilled glass.

MOSCOW MULE

30 ml (1 fl oz) Vodka
½ a lime
Ginger Beer to top
Garnish: slice of lime and mint

• **Build over ice.**

MOSCOW MULE

HARVEY WALLBANGER

45 ml (1½ fl oz) Vodka
125 ml (4 fl oz) orange juice
15 ml (½ fl oz) Vanilla Galliano
Garnish: orange slice and cherry

- Add Vodka and orange juice to glass full of ice and stir. Float Galliano on top of mix and serve.

- Hawaiian bartenders will tell you a visiting Irishman called Harvey pin-balled down the corridor to hotel room after a night out. Hence, he was known as "Harvey Wallbanger".

SCREWDRIVER

45 ml (1½ fl oz) Vodka
45 ml (1½ fl oz) orange juice
Garnish: orange wedge or spiral.

• Build over ice.

Variations

A COMFORTABLE SCREW
Made with 30 ml (1 fl oz) Vodka, 15 ml (½ fl oz) Southern Comfort and topped with orange juice.

A SLOW COMFORTABLE SCREW
Made with the addition of 15 ml (½ fl oz) Sloe Gin.

A LONG SLOW COMFORTABLE SCREW
A longer drink served in a highball glass and topped with orange juice.

A LONG SLOW COMFORTABLE SCREW UP AGAINST A WALL
Add of 15 ml (½ fl oz) Galliano floated on top.

KAMIKAZE

30 ml (1 fl oz) Vodka
30 ml (1 fl oz) Cointreau
30 ml (1 fl oz) fresh lemon juice
1 teaspoon lime cordial
Garnish: lime wheel

- Pour ingredients into a cocktail shaker over ice and shake.

- Strain into chilled glass.

CHOCOLATE MARTINI

60 ml (2 fl oz) Vodka
15 ml (½ fl oz) white Crème de Cacao
Garnish: cocao or chocolate

- Pour ingredients into a cocktail shaker over ice and shake.

- Prepare a cocktail glass with a cocoa powder frosted rim – moistened with Cacao.

- Strain into a chilled martini glass and serve.

This drink is also known as Chocolate Monk.

CHOCOLATE MINT MARTINI
60 ml (2 fl oz) Vodka
30 ml (1 fl oz) white Crème de Cacao
30 ml (1 fl oz) white Crème de menthe

- Prepare a cocktail glass with a cocoa powder frosted rim –moistened with Cacao.

- Pour ingredients into a cocktail shaker over ice and shake. Strain into prepared glass and serve.

WATERMELON MARTINI

60 ml (2 fl oz) Vodka
Dash sugar syrup
Slice of fresh Watermelon (crushed)
Garnish: a wedge of watermelon

- Pour Vodka and sugar into a cocktail shaker over ice then add crushed watermelon.

- Shake well and strain into a chilled martini glass.

VODKA MARTINI

60 ml (2 fl oz) Vodka
15 ml (½ fl oz) Dry Vermouth
Garnish: lemon twist

- Pour Vodka and Vermouth into a mixing glass over ice then stir until liquid is chilled.

- Strain into a chilled martini glass and garnish with a twist of lemon peel then serve.

WHITE RUSSIAN

2 fl oz (60 ml) Vodka
1 fl oz (30 ml) white Crème de Cacao
1 fl oz (30 ml) double (heavy) cream

• Shake all ingredients with ice in a
  shaker and strain into glass.

SALTY DOG

45 ml (1½ fl oz) Vodka
Grapefruit juice, to top
Garnish: grapefruit slice

• Build over ice.

• Straws are generally unnecessary,
  drink the cocktail from the salt rim.

SALTY DOG

GIN

RAFFLES SINGAPORE SLING

30 ml (1 fl oz) Gin
30 ml (1 fl oz) Cherry Brandy
15 ml (½ fl oz) Bénédictine
15 ml (½ fl oz) Cointreau
Dash Angostura Bitters
30 ml (1 fl oz) fresh lime juice
30 ml (1 fl oz) fresh orange juice
30 ml (1 fl oz) pineapple juice
Slice of orange
Sprig of fresh mint
Garnish: slice of pineapple and cherry

- Pour Gin, Brandy, Bénédictine, Cointreau, Bitters and juices into a cocktail shaker over ice.

- Shake and strain into a highball glass over ice.

DRY MARTINI

60 ml (2 oz) Dry Gin
10–15 ml (⅓–½ oz) Dry Vermouth
Garnish: green olives

• Pour Gin and Vermouth into a mixing
  glass over ice then stir until liquid is
  chilled.

• Strain into a chilled martini glass,
  add olives then serve.

DRY MARTINI

DIRTY MARTINI

60 ml (2 oz) Dry Gin
10–15 ml (⅓–½ oz) Dry Vermouth
Add 15 ml (½ fl oz) olive brine
Garnish: green olives

- Pour Gin and Vermouth into a mixing glass over ice and then add olive brine then stir until liquid is chilled.

- Strain into a chilled martini glass, add olives then serve.

DIRTY MARTINI

NEGRONI

20 ml (⅔ fl oz) Campari
20 ml (⅔ fl oz) Sweet Vermouth
20 ml (⅔ fl oz) Gin
Garnish: twist of orange peel and an
  oversized ice cube

- Pour ingredients into mixing glass
  and stir until chilled.

- Strain over oversized ice cube.

- Squeeze orange peel over glass to
  release the juices before dropping
  it in.

TOM COLLINS

30 ml (2 fl oz) lemon juice
60 ml (2 fl oz) Gin
15 ml (½ fl oz) sugar syrup
Soda water
Garnish: serve with a slice of lemon
and cherry

- Put cracked ice, lemon juice, and Gin
in a glass.

- Fill with soda water and stir.

GIMLET

60 ml (2 fl oz) Gin
30 ml (1 fl oz) lime juice
15 ml (½ fl oz) sugar syrup
Garnish: lime wheel

- **Pour ingredients into a cocktail shaker. Shake over ice and pour, then add cubed ice.**

- **This cocktail can also be made using pear juice.**

- **Adjust sugar syrup to taste.**

BLUES MARTINI

15 ml (½ fl oz) Dry Gin
15 ml (½ fl oz) Vodka
Dash Blue Curaçao

- Pour ingredients into a mixing glass over ice and stir gently.

- Strain into a martini glass over a small amount of cracked ice and serve.

BLOODY MARTINI

60 ml (2 fl oz) Gin
Dash Grenadine cordial
7.5 ml (1½ tsp) Dry Vermouth

- Combine the ingredients with cracked ice in a cocktail shaker and shake well.

- Strain into a chilled glass.

GIN SLING

60 ml (2 fl oz) Gin
Dash Grenadine
30 ml (1 fl oz) fresh orange juice
90 ml (3 fl oz) soda water
Maraschino cherry
Garnish: slice of lemon

- Pour Gin, Grenadine and juice into a highball glass over ice.

- Add soda and stir gently.

- Garnish with a cherry and slice of lemon then serve.

GIN SLING

STRAWBERRY FIZZ

60 ml (2 fl oz) Gin
15 ml (½ fl oz) fresh lemon juice
15 ml (½ fl oz) thick cream
1 teaspoon caster sugar
90 ml (3 fl oz) soda Wwater
4 strawberries (crushed)
Garnish: strawberry

- Pour Gin, juice and cream into a cocktail shaker over ice.

- Add sugar and crushed strawberries.

- Shake and strain into a glass over ice.

- Add soda and stir gently.

- Garnish with a strawberry and serve. This drink is also known as Strawberry Blush.

GIN FIZZ

60 ml (2 fl oz) Dry Gin
15 ml (½ fl oz) fresh lemon juice
15 ml (½ fl oz) fresh lime juice
1 teaspoon Caster sugar
White of 1 egg
60 ml (2 fl oz) soda water
Garnish: slice of lemon

- Pour Gin, juices and egg white into a cocktail shaker over ice then add sugar.

- Shake and strain into a highball glass over ice.

- Add soda and stir gently.
  Garnish with a slice of lemon.

- This drink is also known as Silver Fizz.

GIN AND CAMPARI

38 ml (1¼ fl oz) Gin
38 ml (1¼ fl oz) Campari
Garnish: twist of orange peel

- Pour Gin and Campari into a mixing glass over ice.

- Stir and strain into a chilled cocktail glass.

- Twist orange peel above drink and place remainder of peel into drink then serve.

ORANGE BLOSSOM

30 ml (1 fl oz) Gin
45 ml (1½ fl oz) fresh orange juice
Garnish: slice of orange

- Pour Gin and juice into a cocktail shaker over ice.

- Shake and strain into a chilled cocktail glass.

- Garnish with a slice of orange and serve.

ORANGE BLOSSOM

GIN AND TONIC

45 ml (1½ fl oz) Gin
90 ml (3 fl oz) Tonic Water
Garnish: wedge of lime

- Pour Gin into a glass over ice and twist wedge of lime above drink to release juice.

- Stir, add tonic and stir gently. Add spent lime shell and serve.

FLYING DUTCHMAN

60 ml (2 fl oz) Gin
Dash Cointreau

- Pour ingredients into a cocktail shaker over ice and shake.

- Strain into an old-fashioned glass over ice and serve.

BARON COCKTAIL

45 ml (1½ fl oz) Gin
15 ml (½ fl oz) Dry Vermouth
8 ml (¼ fl oz) Cointreau
2 dashes Sweet Vermouth
Garnish: twist of lime peel

- Pour Gin, Vermouths and Cointreau into a mixing glass over ice.

- Stir and strain into a chilled cocktail glass.

- Garnish with lime peel and serve.

ALEXANDRA MARTINI

30 ml (1 fl oz) Gin
30 ml (1 fl oz) Ream
30 ml (1 fl oz) dark Crème de Cacao

- Combine the liquid ingredients with cracked ice in a cocktail shaker and shake well.

- Pour slowly into a chilled cocktail glass.

BOMBAY MARTINI

BOMBAY MARTINI

90 ml (3 fl oz) Gin
Splash Dry Vermouth
Garnish: olive

- Combine liquid ingredients in a mixing glass with ice cubes and stir well.

- Strain into a chilled glass and garnish with the olive.

CHRISTMAS MARTINI

45 ml (1½ fl oz) Gin
7.5 ml (1½ tsp) Vermouth
5 ml (1 tsp) Peppermint Schnapps
Garnish: red and green cocktail onions,

- Combine the liquid ingredients with cracked ice in a cocktail shaker and shake well.

- Strain into a chilled glass and garnish with cocktail onions.

HO HO MARTINI

30 ml (1 fl oz) Gin
30 ml (1 fl oz) Light Rum
7.5 ml (1½ tsp) Dry Vermouth
1 dash Orange Bitters
Garnish: almond-stuffed olive

- Combine the liquid ingredients with cracked ice in a cocktail shaker and shake well.

- Strain into a chilled glass and garnish with the olive.

GREYHOUND

45 ml (1½ fl oz) Dry Gin
150 ml (5 fl oz) grapefruit juice

- **Pour Gin into a highball glass over ice and add juice, stir then serve.**

GREYHOUND

TEQUILA

FROZEN MARGARITA

60 ml (2 fl oz) Tequila
30 ml (1 fl oz) lime juice
15 ml (½ fl oz) Cointreau
Garnish: lime wheel

- Add ingredients to blender over crushed ice and blend until smooth.

MARGARITA

60 ml (2 fl oz) Tequila
30 ml (1 fl oz) lime juice
30 ml (1 fl oz) Cointreau
Garnish: lime wheel on edge of
  glass and salt rim

- Pour ingredients into a
  cocktail shaker over ice and
  shake.

- Strain into chilled glass.

MARGARITA

TEQUILA SUNRISE

30 ml Tequila
1 teaspoon Grenadine
Orange juice, to top
Garnish: orange wheel, a red cherry.

- To obtain the cleanest visual effect, drop Grenadine down the inside of the glass, after topping up with orange juice.

- Dropping Grenadine in the middle creates a fallout effect, detracting from the presentation of the cocktail.

- Best served with chilled, freshly squeezed orange juice.

Variation

VODKA SUNRISE
Replace Tequila with Vodka.

APPLE MARGARITA

30 ml (1 fl oz) White Tequila
30 ml (1 fl oz) Cointreau
60 ml (2 fl oz) apple juice

- Pour ingredients into a cocktail shaker over ice and shake well.

- Strain into a chilled Margarita glass and serve.

APPLE MARGARITA

BERRY MARGARITA

45 ml (1½ fl oz) White Tequila
15 ml (½ fl oz) Cointreau
60 ml (2 fl oz) fresh lime juice
4 fresh strawberries (diced)
Garnish: fresh strawberry

- Prepare a Margarita glass with a sugar-frosted rim.

- Pour Tequila, Cointreau and juice into a blender over a large amount of crushed ice then add diced strawberries.

- Blend until slushy andpour into prepared glass.

- Garnish with a strawberry and serve.

BERRY MARGARITA

CATALINA MARGARITA

45 ml (1½ fl oz) White Tequila
30 ml (1 fl oz) Blue Curaçao
30 ml (1 fl oz) Peach Schnapps
120 ml (4 fl oz) sweet & sour mix

- Pour ingredients into a cocktail shaker over ice and shake well.

- Strain into a chilled Margarita glass and serve.

MANDARIN MARGARITA

45 ml (1½ fl oz) Gold Tequila
20 ml (⅔ fl oz) Mandarine Napoleon
15 ml (½ fl oz) Cointreau
30 ml (1 fl oz) fresh lemon juice
Garnish: slice of fresh orange

- Prepare a Margarita glass with a salt-frosted rim.

- Pour Tequila, Mandarine Napoleon, Cointreau and juice into a blender over cracked ice then blend.

- Strain into prepared glass and garnish with a slice of orange then serve with a short straw.

SHARKARITA

45 ml (1½ fl oz) White Tequila
15 ml (½ fl oz) Cointreau
5 ml (⅙ fl oz) Raspberry Liqueur
30 ml (1 fl oz) fresh lemon juice

- Pour Tequila, Cointreau and juice
  into a blender over a large amount of
  crushed ice then blend until slushy.

- Pour into a chilled Margarita glass
  and gently add Liqueur – do not stir,
  then serve.

SHARKARITA

TALL MARGARITA

45 ml (1½ fl oz) Gold Tequila
15 ml (½ fl oz) Cointreau
23 ml (¾ fl oz) fresh lemon juice
120 ml (4 fl oz) bitter-lemon soda
Garnish: slice of fresh lemon

- Pour Tequila, Cointreau and juice into a cocktail shaker over ice then shake.

- Strain into a tall glass over ice and add bitterlemon soda then stir gently.

- Add more ice to fill the glass and garnish with a slice of lemon.

MANSION MARGARITA

38 ml (1¼ fl oz) Gold Tequila
23 ml (¾ fl oz) Cointreau
23 ml (¾ fl oz) Grand Marnier
38 ml (1¼ fl oz) sweet & sour mix

• Pour ingredients into a cocktail
  shaker over ice and shake well.

• Strain into a Margarita glass half-
  filled with cracked ice and add more
  cracked ice to fill the glass.

MANSION MARGARITA

PINK MARGARITA

45 ml (1½ fl oz) White Tequila
15 ml (½ fl oz) Raspberry Liqueur
5 ml (⅙ fl oz) Grenadine
15 ml (½ fl oz) fresh lemon
  or lime juice
½ egg white

- Prepare a Margarita glass with a salt-frosted rim. Pour ingredients into a cocktail shaker over ice and shake well.

- Strain into prepared glass and serve.

BLACKBERRY MARGARITA

53 ml (1¾ fl oz) White Tequila
15 ml (½ fl oz) Blackberry Schnapps
23 ml (¾ fl oz) fresh lime juice
10 fresh blackberries (diced)
Garnish: 2 fresh blackberries

- Prepare a Margarita glass with a sugar-frosted rim.

- Pour Tequila, Schnapps and juice into a blender over a large amount of crushed ice then add diced blackberries.

- Blend until slushy and pour into prepared glass.

- Garnish with blackberries and serve.

PINK CADILLAC MARGARITA

60 ml (2 fl oz) White Tequila
30 ml (1 fl oz) Cointreau
60 ml (2 fl oz) fresh lime juice
30 ml (1 fl oz) cranberry juice
1 teaspoon sugar syrup

- Pour ingredients into a cocktail shaker over small amount of cracked ice and shake well.

- Pour into a chilled Margarita glass and serve with a short straw.

PINK CADILLAC MARGARITA

CADALAC MARGARITA

60 ml (2 fl oz) Gold Tequila
23 ml (¾ fl oz) Grand Marnier
38 ml (1¼ fl oz) sweet & sour mix
Garnish: wedge of fresh lime

- Prepare a Margarita glass with a salt-frosted rim.

- Pour Tequila, Grand Marnier and sweet & sour mix into a cocktail shaker over ice then shake well.

- Strain into prepared glass and garnish with a wedge of lime then serve.

CADALAC MARGARITA

COCO MARGARITA

38 ml (1¼ fl oz) White Tequila
15 ml (½ fl oz) Coconut Liqueur
45 ml (1½ fl oz) pineapple juice
30 ml (1 fl oz) sweet & sour mix
15 ml (½ fl oz) fresh lime juice
Garnish: slice of fresh pineapple

- Prepare a Margarita glass with a salt-frosted rim.

- Pour Tequila, Liqueur, juices and sweet & sour mix into a cocktail shaker over ice then shake well.

- Strain into prepared glass and garnish with a slice of pineapple then serve with a short straw.

APRICOT MARGARITA

30 ml (1 fl oz) Gold Tequila
30 ml (1 fl oz) Apricot Brandy
45 ml (1½ fl oz) fresh lemon juice
1 teaspoon sugar syrup
Garnish: slice of fresh apricot

- Pour Tequila, Apricot Brandy, juice
  and sugar into a cocktail shaker
  over ice then shake well.

- Strain into a chilled Margarita glass
  and garnish with a slice of apricot
  then serve.

PEACH MARGARITA

30 ml (1 fl oz) Gold Tequila
8 ml (¼ fl oz) Peach Liqueur
15 ml (½ fl oz) fresh lemon juice
½ fresh Peach (diced)

- Prepare a Margarita glass with a sugar-frosted rim.

- Pour Tequila, Liqueur and juice into a blender over a large amount of crushed ice then add diced Peach.

- Blend until slushy and pour into prepared glass then serve.

PEACH MARGARITA

BLACKJACK MARGARITA

45 ml (1½ fl oz) White Tequila
15 ml (½ fl oz) Chambord
15 ml (½ fl oz) Cointreau
120 ml (4 fl oz) fresh lime juice
Garnish: wedge of fresh lime

- Prepare a Margarita glass with a
  salt-frosted rim.

- Pour Tequila, Chambord, Cointreau
  and juice into a cocktail shaker over
  ice then shake well.

- Strain into prepared glass and
  garnish with a wedge of lime then
  serve.

BLACKJACK MARGARITA

JIMPOP'S MARGARITA

60 ml (2 fl oz) Gold Tequila
23 ml (¾ fl oz) Grand Marnier
30 ml (1 fl oz) fresh lime juice

- Prepare a Margarita glass with a salt-frosted rim and half-fill the prepared glass with cracked ice.

- Pour ingredients into a mixing glass over ice and stir well.

- Strain into prepared glass and add more cracked ice to fill the glass then serve.

GREEN IGUANA
MARGARITA

30 ml (1 fl oz) White Tequila
15 ml (½ fl oz) Midori
60 ml (2 fl oz) sweet & sour mix

- Prepare a Margarita glass with a salt-frosted rim.

- Pour ingredients into a blender over a large amount of cracked ice and blend.

- Pour into prepared glass and serve.

GRANRITA

45 ml (1½ fl oz) Gold Tequila
15 ml (½ fl oz) Grand Marnier
30 ml (1 fl oz) fresh lemon juice
Garnish: slice of fresh lemon

- Prepare a Margarita glass with
  a salt-frosted rim and halffill the
  prepared glass with crushed ice.

- Pour Tequila, Grand Marnier and
  juice into a cocktail shaker over ice
  then shake well.

- Strain into prepared glass and add
  more crushed ice to fill the glass
  then stir.

- Garnish with a slice of lemon.

GRANRITA

FUZZY RITA

45 ml (1½ fl oz) Gold Tequila
15 ml (½ fl oz) Cointreau
15 ml (½ fl oz) Peach Schnapps
45 ml (1½ fl oz) fresh lime juice

- Pour ingredients into a mixing glass over ice and stir well.

- Strain into an old-fashioned glass over ice and add more ice to fill the glass then serve.

PASSIONATE RITA

45 ml (1½ fl oz) Gold Tequila
30 ml (1 fl oz) Passionfruit Liqueur
15 ml (½ fl oz) fresh lime juice

- Pour ingredients into a cocktail shaker over ice and shake well.

- Strain into a chilled cocktail glass and serve.

PASSIONATE RITA

MIDORI MARGARITA

30 ml (1 fl oz) White Tequila
30 ml (1 fl oz) Midori
45 ml (1½ fl oz) fresh lemon juice
1 teaspoon sugar syrup
Garnish: slice of fresh lime

- Pour Tequila, Midori, juice and sugar into a cocktail shaker over ice then shake well.

- Strain into a chilled Margarita glass and garnish with a slice of lime then serve.

FROZEN ITALIAN MARGARITA

Lime or lemon slices
Salt
180 ml (6 fl oz) frozen lemonade
  concentrate
90 ml (3 fl oz) Tequila
60 ml (2 fl oz) Amaretto
30 ml (1 fl oz) Cointreau
Garnish: lime or lemon Slices

- Rub the Margarita glass rim with a lime or lemon slice and frost with salt.

- Put all liquid ingredients and 1 cup ice in a blender and blend until slushy. Pour into the glass, garnish with the remaining lime or lemon slice.

FROZEN MARGARITAS WITH LIME

1 lime, cut into slices
Sugar
380 ml (13 fl oz) sweet & sour mix
120 ml (4 fl oz) Tequila
75 ml (2½ fl oz) papaya nectar
75 ml (2½ fl oz) guava nectar
60 ml (2 fl oz) coconut cream
Garnish: slices of lime

- Rub 6 glass rims with lime slices and frost with sugar.

- Combine the remaining ingredients in a blender with 8 ice cubes and process until well blended.

- Pour into the glasses and garnish each with slices of lime.

WHISKEY

WHISKY SOUR

60 ml (1½ fl oz) Scotch Whisky
30 ml (1 fl oz) lemon juice
15 ml (½ fl oz) sugar syrup
½ egg white
Garnish: red cherry and slice of lemon

- Add ingredients to shaker and shake vigorously for 10–15 seconds without ice.

- Add ice to shaker and shake. Double strain over fresh ice.

Variation

AMARETTO SOUR
Replace the Whisky with Amaretto.

GODFATHER

1 fl oz (30 ml) Scotch Whisky
1 fl oz (30 ml) Amaretto
Garnish: orange wheel

• Mix together and then pour into
  glass over ice and stir.

OLD-FASHIONED SCOTCH

Angostura Bitters
1 sugar cube
30 ml (1 fl oz) Scotch Whisky
Soda water
Garnish: slice of lemon
Garnish: slice of orange

- Splash Bitters evenly over sugar cube before adding ice and Scotch. Top up with soda water.

- Garnish with the slice of lemon and orange.

RUSTY NAIL

30 ml (1 fl oz) Scotch Whisky
30 ml (1 fl oz) Drambuie
Garnish: lemon twist

- Build over ice. Garnish with the
  lemon.

SHOOTERS

MARGARITA SHOOTER

15 ml (½ fl oz) Cointreau
15 ml (½ fl oz) Gold Tequila
10 ml (⅓ fl oz) fresh lemon juice
5 ml (⅙ fl oz) fresh lime juice

• Layer ingredients in order given into
  a shot glass and serve as a shooter.

JAGERITA

10 ml (⅓ fl oz) Jägermeister
10 ml (⅓ fl oz) Gold Tequila
10 ml (⅓ fl oz) fresh lime juice

- **Pour ingredients in order given gently into a shot glass – do not stir, then serve as a shooter.**

JAGERITA

SANGRITA NO.2

30 ml (1 fl oz) tomato juice (chilled)
Dash fresh lemon juice
Pinch of black pepper (ground)

- Pour juices into a mixing glass over ice and add black pepper to the mixing glass then stir well.

- Strain into a chilled shot glass and serve; to be slowly sipped.

SANGRITA NO.2

SANGRITA

30 ml (1 fl oz) Gold Tequila or
   White Tequila
30 ml (1 fl oz) tomato juice (chilled)
Dash fresh lemon juice
Pinch of black pepper (ground)

- This drink is served with the Tequila in its own shot glass and the other ingredients are mixed together and served in a separate chilled shot glass.

- The drinker takes a sip of the Tequila and then a sip from the other shot glass until all is consumed. First pour gold or White Tequila into a shot glass.

- Then pour juices into a mixing glass over ice followed by black pepper.

- Stir well and strain into a chilled shot glass then serve together with the Tequila in the (unchilled) shot glass.

SANGRITA

SMURF TOWN

15 ml (½ fl oz) Blue Curaçao
15 ml (½ fl oz) Peach Schnapps
Fresh whipped cream, to serve
5 drops Grenadine

- Pour the Curaçao and Schnapps into a shot glass. Float a small spoonful of cream on top. Drop the Grenadine on the cream.

GOLDEN FLASH

2 tsp (10 ml) Amaretto
2 tsp (10 ml) Triple sec
2 tsp (10 ml) Sambuca

- Layer the ingredients in a shot glass working from top to bottom of the ingredient's list.

- Allow each to settle before adding the next.

GREEN APPLE

30 ml (1 fl oz) Southern Comfort
5 ml–1 tsp (5 ml) Midori – (⅙ fl oz)
1 tsp (5 ml) – (⅙ fl) oz sweet & sour
  mix

- Pour all the ingredients into a mixing glass over ice and stir.

- Strain into a chilled shot glass.

G-SPOT

15 ml (½ fl oz) Chambord
15 ml (½ fl oz) Southern Comfort
15 ml (½ fl oz) fresh orange juice

- Pour the ingredients into a cocktail shaker over ice and shake.

- Strain into a chilled glass.

FIFTH AVENUE

15 ml (½ fl oz) dark Crème de Cacao
15 ml (½ fl oz) Apricot Brandy
15 ml (½ fl oz) single (light) cream (chilled)

- Layer the ingredients in a shot glass working from top to bottom of the ingredient's list.

- Allow each to settle before adding the next.

BRAIN HAEMORRHAGE

30 ml (1 fl oz) Peach Schnapps
5 ml (1 tsp) Baileys
3 dashes Grenadine coridal

- Pour each drink in order into the glass, allowing each to settle before carefully adding the next. Do not stir.

LAVA LAMP

1½ tsp (7.5 ml) Kahlúa
1½ tsp (7.5 ml) Strawberry Liqueur
1½ tsp (7.5 ml) Frangelico
1½ tsp (7.5 ml) Baileys
3 drops Advocaat

- Pour the Kahlúa, Strawberry Liqueur and Frangelico into a shot glass but do not stir. Allow to settle. Layer the Baileys on top.

- Drop in the Advocaat.

MEXICAN CHICKEN

1 fresh egg
30 ml (1 fl oz) Tequila
Dash Tabasco sauce

- Crack the egg into a liqueur glass and add the Tequila.

- Add the sauce and serve.

JELLYFISH

15 ml (½ fl oz) Amaretto
15 ml (½ fl oz) dark Crème de Cacao
7.5 ml (1½ tsp) Baileys
3 drops Grenadine

- Pour the Amaretto and Cacao into a shot glass allowing the Amaretto to settle before adding the Cacao. Carefully add the Baileys and then add the Grenadine.

HARD ROCK

2 tsp (10 ml) Midori
2 tsp (10 ml) Vodka
2 tsp (10 ml) Baileys

- Layer the ingredients in order in the glass and serve.

ESTONIAN FOREST FIRE

30 ml (1 fl oz) Vodka
12 drops Tabasco Sauce
Garnish: 1 kiwi fruit

- **Pour the Vodka and Tabasco into a shot glass.**

- **Stir and serve with a kiwi fruit, which should be eaten after the shot has been consumed.**

CREME-BASED COCKTAILS

ALEXANDER

30 ml (1 fl oz) Gin
30 ml (1 fl oz) white Crème de Cacao
30 ml (1 fl oz) heavy (double) cream
Ground (powdered) nutmeg

- Shake all the liquid ingredients with ice and strain into a cocktail glass. Sprinkle nutmeg on top.

ALEXANDER

BRIGHT EYES

30 ml (1 fl oz) Vodka
30 ml (1 fl oz) white Crème de Cacao
30 ml (1 fl oz) Strawberry Liqueur
30 ml (1 fl oz) heavy (double) cream
30 ml (1 fl oz) Banana Liqueur
6 ripe strawberries
Garnish: chocolate flakes

• Blend all the liquid ingredients with
  five strawberries and ice, then pour
  into the glass. Garnish with the
  remaining strawberry and sprinkle
  chocolate flakes on top.

PINK POODLE

30 ml (1 fl oz) Campari
30 ml (1 fl oz) Dry Gin
30 ml (1 fl oz) double (heavy) cream
4 strawberries

- Blend all the ingredients with ice
  and pour into the glass.

PINK POODLE

SOMBRERO

45 ml (1½ fl oz) Coffee Liqueur
30 ml double (1 fl oz) (heavy) cream

• Shake all the ingredients with ice
  and strain into a chilled Brandy
  balloon glass.

SWEET LADY JANE

15 ml (½ fl oz) white Curaçao
30 ml (1 fl oz) Strawberry Liqueur
30 ml (1 fl oz) double (heavy) cream
15 ml (½ fl oz) orange juice
15 ml (½ fl oz) coconut cream
Garnish: 1 strawberry
Garnish: chocolate flakes, to sprinkle

- Shake all liquid ingredients with ice and strain into the Champagne saucer.

- Garnish with a strawberry on the side of the glass and sprinkle chocolate flakes on top.

MULTIPLE ORGASM

30 ml (1 fl oz) Baileys
30 ml (1 fl oz) Cointreau
30 ml (1 fl oz) heavy (double) cream
Garnish: 1 red cherry
Garnish: ground (powdered) cinnamon

- Build the liquid over ice cubes in the glass and stir.

- Garnish with the cherry and cinnamon.

DRINKS WITH FIZZ

CHAMPAGNE COCKTAIL

1 sugar cube
6 drops Angostura Bitters
15 ml (½ fl oz) Cognac
120 ml (4 fl oz) Champagne
Garnish: 1 cherry

• Soak the sugar cube in the
  Angostura Bitters in the flute before
  adding the Cognac, then top with
  Champagne. Drop the cherry into
  the glass.

DEATH IN THE AFTERNOON

15 ml (½ fl oz) Pernod
120 ml (4 fl oz) Champagne

• Pour the Pernod into glass then fill
  with chilled Champagne.

BOMBAY PUNCH

30 ml (1 fl oz) Cognac
15 ml (½ fl oz) Dry Sherry
15 ml (½ fl oz) Cointreau
15 ml (½ fl oz) Maraschino Liqueur
15 ml (½ fl oz) lemon juice
Sparkling Wine
Garnish: 1 red cherry

- Blend the first 5 ingredients with ice and pour into the glass.

- Top up with Sparkling Wine and garnish with the red cherry.

SANGRIA

1 bottle Red Wine
2 fl oz (60 ml) Brandy
2 fl oz (60 ml) White Rum
2 fl oz (60 ml) Cointreau
4 cups (1¾ pints/1 litre)
Orange juice
2 tsp (10 ml) sugar
Selection of chopped fruit
4 cups of ice cubes
Garnish: orange

- Pour all ingredients into punch bowl with 4 cups ice cubes and stir well.

- Glass tip: jug or punch bowl

- Serve in cocktail glasses.

BRAZIL COCKTAIL

45 ml (1½ fl oz) Dry Sherry
45 ml (1½ fl oz) Dry Vermouth
Dash of Angostura Bitters
2.5 ml (½ tsp) Ouzo

• Place all the ingredients in the
mixing glass with cracked ice,
stir well and then strain into the
cocktail glass.

SPRITZER

90 ml (3 fl oz) Dry White Wine
Soda water
Garnish: slice of lime

- Pour chilled Wine into the glass,
  then top up with chilled soda water,
  no ice.

- Add a slice of lime to the edge
  of the glass.

APPLE PUNCH

8 Apples, cored and sliced
Juice of 1 lemon
40 ml (1¼ fl oz) sugar
120 ml (4 fl oz) Calvados
2 bottles White Wine
1 bottle soda water
1 bottle Champagne
Serving bowl: 1 large punch bowl

- Place apples in the punch bowl, drizzle lemon juice over and sprinkle with sugar.

- Refrigerate for 3–4 hours.

- Add the Calvados and White Wine and stir well.

- Add the soda water, Champagne and 4 cups ice cubes.

- Serve in cocktail glasses or Champagne flutes.

COLD DUCK

2 bottles White Wine
1 bottle sparkling Wine
2 lemon peel spirals, to garnish
Serving bowl: 1 large punch bowl

- Pour all ingredients into punch bowl with 2 cups ice cubes and stir well.

- Serve in Champagne flutes or wine glasses.

MELON PUNCH

½ bottle Melon Liqueur
½ bottle Vodka
1¾ pints (1 litre) lemonade
475 ml (16 fl oz) pineapple juice
Selection of chopped fruit
Serving bowl: large punch bowl or jug

- Pour all ingredients into punch bowl with 2 cups ice cubes and stir well.

- Serve in White Wine glasses.

MELON PUNCH

KIWI PUNCH

6 kiwi fruit, peeled and diced
2 nectarines, diced
30 ml (1 fl oz) Dark Rum
1 bottle dry White Wine
1¾ pints (1 litre) lemonade
Serving bowl: 1 large punch bowl

- Place the fruit into the punch bowl, pour the Rum over the fruit, then cover and refrigerate for about 1 hour.

- Add Wine and stir well. Add 4 cups ice cubes, then top up with the lemonade. Serve in wine glasses or punch mugs.

RASPBERRY LIME PUNCH

450 g (1 lb) raspberries
1 lime, sliced
40 g (1¾ oz) caster (superfine) sugar
2 bottles Rosé wine
3 bottles Champagne
Serving bowl: punch bowl or jug

- Place raspberries and lime slices into punch bowl.

- Sprinkle sugar over the fruit, cover and refrigerate for about half an hour. Add Rosé and stir well.

- Add 4 cups ice cubes, then top up with the Champagne.

- Serve in cocktail glasses.

HOT DRINKS

BEDROOM FARCE

30 ml (1 fl oz) Dark Rum
15 ml (½ fl oz) Bourbon
10 ml (2 tsp) Galliano
120 ml (4 fl oz) hot chocolate
60 ml (2 fl oz) double (heavy) cream
2.5 ml (½ tsp) grated (shredded)
    dark (bittersweet) chocolate

- Pour first three ingredients into
  an Irish coffee glass, then add hot
  chocolate.

- Carefully spoon cream on top, and
  sprinkle with the grated chocolate.

CALYPSO COFFEE

Slice of orange
Sugar
45 ml (1½ fl oz) Dark Rum
Hot coffee
Whipped cream

- **Rub rim of glass with orange and frost with sugar. Pour Rum into the glass and fill to within ½ in (15 mm) of the top with the hot coffee.**

- **Cover the surface with whipped cream.**

BAILEYS IRISH COFFEE

30 ml (1 fl oz) Baileys
5 ml (1 tsp) brown sugar
Hot coffee
Whipped cream
Chocolate flakes, to decorate

- Pour Baileys into the glass and stir in the brown sugar. Fill to within ½ in (15 mm) of top with hot coffee.

- Cover with whipped cream, then top with chocolate flakes.

GIN TODDY

1 sugar cube
60 ml (2 fl oz) Gin
Slice of lemon, to garnish
Garnish: ground (powdered) nutmeg

- Place the sugar cube in the glass,
  pour over ½ cup (120 ml) hot water
  and stir well, then add Gin.

- Float the lemon slice on top and
  sprinkle over nutmeg.

GIN TODDY

HOT BRANDY ALEXANDER

30 ml (1 fl oz) Brandy
30 ml (1 fl oz) dark Crème de Cacao
120 ml (4 fl oz) hot (but not boiling) milk
Garnish: whipped cream, to decorate
Garnish: chocolate flakes, to decorate

- **Pour all the ingredients except for the cream and chocolate into a heated mug.**

- **Top with whipped cream and sprinkle with chocolate flakes.**

HOT WHISKY TODDY

1 sugar cube
60 ml (2 fl oz) Scotch Whisky
Garnish: slice of lemon

- **Put sugar into glass, pour in ⅔ cup (150 ml) boiling water, then add Whisky and stir.**

- **Decorate with a lemon slice.**

INDEX

First published in 2024 by New Holland Publishers
Sydney

Level 1, 178 Fox Valley Road, Wahroonga, NSW 2076, Australia

newhollandpublishers.com

A record of this book is held at the National Library of Australia.

ISBN 9781760796846

Managing Director: Fiona Schultz
Designer: Andrew Davies
Production Director: Arlene Gippert
Printed in China

Keep up with New Holland Publishers:

NewHollandPublishers
@newhollandpublishers